Still Breathing

poems by Antoinette Voûte Roeder

For Pat and Carl,
with god's blessings
Antoinette Voûte Roeder
Nov. 2010

apocryphile press
BERKELEY, CA

Apocryphile Press
1700 Shattuck Ave #81
Berkeley, CA 94709
www.apocryphile.org

Printed in the United States of America.
ISBN 1-933993-79-0

To Michael

Acknowledgments

"Sept. 11, 2001" was previously published in *Presence,* the Journal of Spiritual Directors International, October 2002, volume 8, #3.

"The Witness" was previously published in slightly different form in *Presence,* the Journal of Spiritual Directors International, February 2005, volume 11, #1.

"The Path" was previously published in slightly different form in *The Merton Journal: Journal of the Thomas Merton Society of Great Britain and Ireland,* Advent 2007, volume 14, #2.

I want to thank Nancy Roeder with all my heart for her careful and compassionate reading of the manuscript, her many helps and encouragements.

Also, my thanks and appreciation to my Contemplative Writers Group.

The cover photo of a sunset in Kananaskis Country is by Michael Thomas Roeder.

Author's photo taken by Michael Thomas Roeder.

"God is exhale."
—Aaron Jeffrey Cuffee

Table of Contents

Epilogue

To the Reader

Poetry is a vast container. It can hold every experience, every emotion imaginable. Better than that, you will find yourself "met" in poetry. At some point you may stumble into a poem and know the thrill of being met as an *aha* moment. There is a recognition, a being known by way of the poem, evoking a response like, "Yes, that is exactly how it is." A poem can be intensely relational.

I like to think of poetry as a delicious conspiracy, a conspiracy between reader and poem, each requiring the other. A poem not read is a musical score not played. It lives in the heart and mind of the poet/composer but it is only half a life. The poem, though having a particular focus and thrust when written, keeps its secrets even from the poet. That mystery makes possible many different interpretations. The reader who stays with a poem over several years may find her own perception of it evolving. All times we bring our own experience to the poem which, in a sense, changes it. That is the poem's mettle, its vitality, and its flexibility.

Poetry is a process of exploration and discovery. We find ourselves seeking meaning and relevance at one time, beauty and contentment at another, comfort, or the expression of our anger and impotence.

Oddly enough, we find what we are looking for not only in the words and images but also in the spaces between, the punctuation, the sudden drop-off into a new stanza, the way the poem is placed on the page, in capitalization and italics. Everything in a poem speaks. It is such an intensified form of communication. One does not read poetry to get to the end of the book. Poems are morsels meant to be tasted and chewed thoughtfully. One could spend a lifetime with just one poem.

Finally, poetry starts with the breath, as in meditation. It is punctuated breath, colored breath, textured breath. And when it is, it may land you right in the middle of this inordinately rich, beautiful, and painful world.

I. Yesterday, Today, and Tomorrow

Orchid

Saber-toothed calypso,
tiny tiger of the forest,
grins its yellow-fringed grin,
reveals a pin-striped cup,
crown of purple spikes:
royalty
easily overlooked.

Rose

Tightly folded petals
hold its secrets close.
Bred by gardeners
age after age
this complex web
of shadow and depth
exists to be sniffed,
to be brushed against skin,
and simply to gaze upon.

Delicate,
strong,
silk upon silk,
a rose is a story
unto itself.
Imagine wild English gardens,
blooms drooping, heavy with rain;
a large bouquet in an antique vase
gracing a quiet drawing room.

Roses, redolent of beauty
in a time that has forgotten
just what beauty is.

kinnikinnick

you of the mantra-
like name:

a tiny bell
gathered into
a five-petaled
crimson kiss

by late summer magic,
metamorphosed
to small explosions
fireballs
blushing beneath
leathery leaves.

The Gardens

Morning in the gardens
and there are so few about
that a stroll is meditation
to the sibilant sound of water
and ebullient song of birds.

Awareness grows within me
of a seamless ebb and flow
between the garden and myself.
I am not it, it is not me
this garden and its varied life
nor are we in the least alike,
and yet, and yet...

I've lost the need to grasp
the tulips, hold the cineraria,
print their beauty and their fragrance
on an inner tablet lest I lose
this moment and its joy.

Nothing rises to disturb
the life that here we breathe and
may it ever be so, may the freedom
that I share today with all that grows
around me be what lasts.

Bees

Who would ever have surmised
that those striped and furry bodies,
tiny tigers of wind and pollen,
held the balance of our lives
between their hairy little legs?

Bees are disappearing, swarms of
them have gone without a trace.
Without their work in field and orchard
autumn apples will be but a juicy

memory on our tongues. Almonds,
peppers, peas, and beans will never grace
our plates again. Think of spring robbed
of color. Pink and frothy cherry trees, like
a bride become a widow; painters, poets,
visionaries, dressed in black.

Never in our wildest dreams
has the bee assumed such stature
as it does in its demise.

Shall we rally, march upon
the powers that dictate and
uphold monoculture farming,
widespread spray of pesticides, and

genetic engineering, that which shackles
nature's free-flow in the generative
seed? Will we stand up for the bees?

Shall we stand up for ourselves?

Redwood

Rising redwood
meets the rippled
awning sky, trunk
of nutmeg, deeply
furrowed, aging face
of a powerful life.

I cannot pierce its
maze of branches, mat
of needles, but my glance
can hold the tree
in its entirety.

All at once this giant
plucks me off the
ground, enfolds my self,
my soul and I am amber
core and golden sap
and life, whirling
inside, cones exploding
outside, tall, tall, strong,
strong, spinning higher,
rooting deeper.

Coming back I wonder how
one could ever lay an axe,
open such a vein, tear
one's own heart
out.

Real and Alive

I've always honored
the "given" of trees:
their shelter, their beauty,
their dappled shade,
and more than that,
what they are in themselves.

I respect their age,
their girth, their laborious
growth, their stalwart withstanding
of every season, their
inability to protest.

I suffer with their
insensitive pruning and with
their wounds, oozing sap. So
when she said, "The day they came
to cut down the spruces I could
not watch," I sympathized.

But then, we wanted to plant
a new tree. Oh, what a flap!
It might grow too tall,
too wide, it might shed,
bear fruit, make a mess,
in other words, it might be
real and alive. And how would we
manage the real and alive?

Don't we humans do the same?
We grow tall, perhaps wide,
bear fruit, make a mess.
Why is it only *we* have that right?

Cedars

Strong winds grow
in island cedars,
hurl through shawling
branches, drop their
voices on descent
and slip into a closely
woven web of roots,
earth-bound,
perfectly
at rest.

Nothing, not the slightest
breath is lost in this
economy.

Heaven

Heaven will smell like
a west coast forest when sun
has been on it a while.

When cedars and hemlocks
release their perfume, with
rose-twigged dogwoods
crowding beneath and
maples weaving in and
out and orchids, bunchberries,
wild rhododendrons, primeval
ferns and thick padded moss,
other-world fungi riding
the backs of long-rotten logs and
last year's needles soft underfoot.

Heaven is here,
not something to wait for,
in this west coast forest.

Along the Gorge

Corrugated trunks,
long-fingered fronds
sloping greenly
to dark earth.
Ancient cedars.

Complex web,
moss-laden branches
weirdly dancing
against the sky.
Garry oaks.

Placid water
bursts open.
Shaking out
royal robes
the cormorant raises
his princely head.

Nature's forms,
no straight lines.
Long slow curve
of bay, of inlet, of the
swan's elegant neck.

In the presence
of mist-shrouded hills
the heart grows silent.
Old magic.

Three Haikus

Hills gallop away
in the mist, in a rushing
to the patient sea

Shower of petals
from a cherry blossom tree
Sweetest of all rain

Indigo storm-clothed
mountains never appear from
behind a silk screen

Origins

At the inlet, land
flows into sea, creeps
below it. Mist drifts
over lapping waves.

Somewhere deep beneath
the surface flows another
sea, a molten fire never
still, original earth still
with us, untamed,
inflamed.

Nothing's ever
what it seems.

Hospitality

It is as if the universe
had been expecting us,
he said.*

Like the father's feast
for the prodigal, earth,
air, and water conjured
up their finest for us.

We never guessed their
tender balance, lived
as if abundance has no
limits, claiming need when

it was greed, to forage,
flail, and beat into
submission all the earth.

Now she cringes,
shrinks away from us,
marked by the demands we've made,
as one by one her creatures vanish.

We will be the sole heirs
left to fight for what remains,
leaving her a ruined citadel,
monument to our lack
of gratitude, of generosity.

*Freeman Dyson, physicist

Trout

Under the bridge
in water so clear
you could count each pebble
a ballet is taking place.

Over dips in the gravel,
hardy swimmers hang
suspended, hundreds of
sleek fat trout.

At a moment known to the
female alone, she flips on her
side and releases a jet, a milky
cloud. Bigger males hover, waiting,
fending off alien suitors.
As they move in with thrashing
tails, they fertilize the eggs.

Over and over and surely
exhausting, this frenzied labor
repeats itself. No body-to-body
or fin-to-fin, no loving gaze
or tender touch between them, yet
no one watching could possibly doubt
the ecstasy of this dance.

Gone

"Gone fishing."
Not likely.
Not in 2050.

Catfish, monkfish, swordfish
gone.
Pickerel, mackerel, turbot
gone.
To say nothing of tuna,
salmon, and sea bass,
scallops, shrimp, and crabs.

What about gulls, osprey,
pelicans, cormorants?
They depend on fish for food.
What about bears
who stalk the river
when salmon are running,
and fertilize forests
with their remains?

What about us?
Gone from our tables
but perhaps even worse,
gone from our lives,
our lips, our language.

What does it mean then
"Be ye fishers of men?"
What was that sign
carved into a wall or

drawn in the sand
to show The Way?

And Jonah was caught
in the belly of *what*?

Gone.
Fishing.
Going,
going,
....

Lab Report

Let's face it.
The experiment has failed
The human earns
a great big zero.

Despite Plato, Jesus,
Gautama, Rumi,
Shakespeare, Mozart, Einstein,
(did I mention Rembrandt?) we
have forfeited the gift, life
on planet earth. In a couple of

centuries we have sent
the planet back to primal storm,
fire, and deluge with our avarice,
our greed, with our totally stupendous
lack of understanding that the whole
works only when its parts are healthy and

guess what? *We* are the sickest part.
Think of it. Or better yet look
to the heart, the human body,
every body, feathered, furry, or
dressed in leaves. Fall on your knees.
Regard the intricacies, elegance, efficiency!
Looking, however, is not

our forte nor can we claim awareness
and gratitude is a foreign word.
The earth mourns as we speed
full throttle ahead to the denouement of
this, the human drama, the experiment
that failed.

Deep Rain

After days of searing heat
and nights allowing no escape
a tapestry of cloud unrolls
and moisture drops like manna
in the wilderness.

Its sound, the weight of rain
cleaving to leaf,
rolling off onto another
in its arbitrary path
nourishes me as surely
as it quickens life outside.

Rain talks in steady tones.

> *I will not overwhelm you,*
> *see? Slowly, carefully, I part*
> *the grass, the bushes,*
> *softening soil and only then*
> *penetrate your roots*
> *that you may take me in,*
> *absorb me as much*
> *as you can for now.*

When rain comes like this
it is like first love,
listening, waiting
for the beloved's consent.

Clouds

Olympian peaks stack the
horizon, shaded with indigo
valleys and smoky pearl
summits, recently tinted by
a rising sun. How they cluster

and clutter the world's edge,
traveling ever so slowly, their mission
mysterious but seemingly one
of surrounding, encircling, embracing.

I stand in their midst. The morning
is new. And all for us,
for me.

Olympics

Every day
the sky invites
their snowy faces

Every day
their mass, their
muscle wraps itself
in folded cloud

Every day
their mystery safe

To Air

Has anyone yet written
a psalm in praise of air?

Invisible except when stirring
sweet foliage of trees and

in that blue, blind canopy.
Not heard, not felt,
she quickens, breathes, makes
possible all life.

Air is surely the most
humble: serving, carrying,
highly tolerant, never denying
and never calling
attention to herself except

of course when in short
supply, when darkened by
pollution, poisoned by
neglect.

Air is generous and
self-giving, always there
for us. Of all God's creatures,
let us praise air. Without her,
we are not.

Serpent

I was just lingering
already full to the brim
with warm sun gleaming off
the water when a slim, lithe

ribbon flowed onto the rock
wall, fluid self feeling into every
unevenness, testing this small
patch of world and just as quietly
slipping out of sight again and I
the only one to attend.

Oh, I would have held
that moment of the other,
life so singular and amazing,
forever if I could.

Yesterday, Today, and...

Yesterday
a garter snake
twin gold stripes, bright band
whips across the path
so swift, so lithe
so elegant

Today
a single cormorant
rides reflected rooftops on
the lake

Always something...

August in Kananaskis

August grows tipsy in its final days
teetering on the brink, all but falling
into September. Its wide blue sky
holds far-from-serious clouds. They
seem to have lost all sense of direction,
lingering as they do.

Under the shadowy shoulders
of Mt. Kidd, a wealth of emerald alders,
tiny cones tousled by the breeze, luxuriates
at the foot of poplars already burned
to a brassy tinge. Asters stand nodding,
some dressed in autumn's woolly caps,
some still wearing a mauve fringe
clustered around a yellow heart.
Strawberry leaves have crimsoned
though an occasional plant, still green,
blooms wholly out of season.
Its bright white flower looks
astonished.

The year is turning
turning slowly
toward its lowest ebb,
leaving a trail of dazzling days,
bronzed afternoons, sudden cool
evenings that chill
our dreams.

Take one deep breath

Take one deep breath of autumn

Fill your mouth
with all its color

Sip on sun-spilled
grasses, crown yourself
with aspen leaves or
balsam poplar, maple
if you're lucky

Let the pale September sky
land right in your eyes

Taste the ripeness
Eat the air

Autumn is so short.
Like life.

Winter Tree

This afternoon
   on the final day
   of September
I look up to see
   a winter tree.
Its few remaining leaves
   worried by wind,
release their tenuous grasp
   with each gust.
   The wind,
indifferent to their plight,
will have it totally stripped
   by night.
The trunk and branches,
scarred and twisted,
are nearly fully exposed
under a wintry sky.

Today she has a foretaste,
 just the appetizer
 of what awaits.

Disappeared

Today we walked above
the river, shrunk to serpentine
proportions, slim and quiet in
comparison with last spring when it
roared and foamed beside us. Then,

as now, we climbed above it and
encountered clumps of orchids, rare
calypsos, small and marching bravely
up the river bank. Now there is no sign
that these exotic flowers ever grew
here. Not a leaf or stem remains.

For every thing there is
a season: orchids,
humans, glaciers.
Even for the earth.

Pyramid Lake

On the first day of October
the earth has tumbled
into winter's arms,
though winter was a stranger
yesterday.

Yesterday
was still September
—that mild and amiable month—
which dithers between
fall and summer,
truly not knowing
where it belongs.

On the lake's edge
the plaited dark trunks
of water birches hold
their ragged bouquets
of rosy leaves like a fan
while the burnt orange crowns
of the balsam poplars
cast their warm light
on the rippling waves.

Low afternoon sun
is unable to warm us.
The icy wind off
this high mountain lake
feeds us mouthfuls of winter
on October's first day.

Following Robert Frost...

In the footsteps of Frost
I am a swinger of birches,
that is to say,
my heart goes out
to aspens and poplars
in full leaf, bent double
with their loads of snow.

Shin-deep in drifts
I wade off trail
to tug at the crowns
of slender young trees
and watch them pop up
releasing showers
of snow I spring
aside to evade.

When sun pierces clouds
and sends shivers of light
through the snow-shrouded valley,
she works with ease.
One by one, branches break free.
Nature needs no help from me.

Beyond

I've hiked this hill
countless times but
today is different.

Halfway up I stop
to ponder the gracious curve
of the path ahead, aspens
leaning toward their
cousins on the opposite side.

Strange to be so mesmerized
by a leaf-strewn path
bending away, in another
season, hushed with snow.

This bit of trail could
be any trail and though
I know just where it leads,
I don't. I teeter on a threshold
between worlds. In time

everything shakes out to this:
a simple path rounding up
a hill, disappearing out
of sight.

Frost

Morning frost
releases leaves that
rain down drop
by drop within
this tightly woven copse
of aspens. Silently,
privately, they fall.

With the rumble of
distant traffic a smudge
on the stillness, here
in this modest display
of autumn, life does
what she does, trysting
with death, making
her yearly exchange.

Winter Swim

Water parts quietly as I make my way
  with   long   smooth   strokes
through glimmering green. Like pieces of a jigsaw puzzle,
  small charcoal clouds hang haphazardly
from the deep mauve pre-dawn sky.

Profound silence blends with
solitude blends with me.

A solitary raven slips over
the mountain crying the colors of dawn
as ground-hugging mist stalks the valley below
and coyotes raise their voices somewhere
across the frozen lake, deep in the trees.
Sun's light washes over the sky
consecrating every thing in its flow.

Enchanted world.
Ordinary world.

a heated outdoor pool
at a mountain lodge

Bosque del Apache

Sun slides closer to
the world's edge as
an apricot sky breaks
open and ranges of purple
hills bear silent witness to
strand upon strand of
sandhill cranes descending,
floating down to winter fields.

It's raining snowgeese,
snowing clouds of geese,
white to silver, catching
the light, thousands of them,
thickly crowded, voices
clashing and competing
in the quickly gathering dusk.

A coyote struts, oblivious,
across an open field and
a great horned owl
bends and bows in
a twiggy old tree,
calling sadly as a two-thirds
moon climbs the sky.

The wild world has not vanished
yet.

Bosque del Apache, the wintering grounds of migratory birds in New Mexico

Advent Fantasy

Mid-afternoon on the first
of December. An old, cold sun
winks weakly through trees.

Wind blisters our faces and
scours the snow, sending up eddies
of powder before us.

Ours are the first tracks,
or so we think, when twin-lobed
hoof prints draw alongside.

Then they appear from out
of the forest: the elegant deer,
the stout snow-shoe hare,
a golden coyote, a lumbering moose.

Ahead and above, waxwings flit,
black masks flashing. Companionably silent
we creatures of earth stride together
toward the light.

Apophasis

The silent forest parts
for those who come
on cushioned feet; for
those who've lost their need
to own, to grasp, to cling;
for those who can no longer separate
themselves from every thing that is;
most of all for those whose language
dies upon their lips. They've traveled much
too far to name the small snow's downward
drift. To disappear with it would be enough.

Hoarfrost

Two days of hoarfrost.
Two full days.

The low and lazy sun
curls around each downy
twig, each frozen bough,
turning it unbearably bright.
Jeweled baubles hang from
stenciled brush of pine.
Earth is all shininess.

Temperatures have dwindled
to far below freezing. They no
longer remember warm.
Even so, the sun's lackluster
wattage thins the delicate
rime on branches, licks it up
crystal by crystal.

So would I, if I could and be
turned into one exquisite moment
of star-bright, star-white tree.

All Sentient Beings

When the world freezes shut
living things go into hiding.

The young box elder in our yard
clamps its roots in stony earth.
Icy winds assail its trunk.
Sculpted snow banks grip it close,
its wiry branches stitch the sky,
a charcoal sketch of various greys.

Somewhere in that slender stalk
do juices flow, does energy rise
to the thrill of sun? Does she
find sustenance in her solitude?

Locked into this patch of turf,
she stands in silence, all her
liveliness contained.

I would like to be so beautiful,
be content with so little, be so
steady and so constant
in this friendless season.

Buddhists pray in company of and for all sentient beings, not just humans

Wild Cousins

Evening falls early
in a high mountain forest
padded with snow.
Flakes have whirled
all day long in a wind
that tussled the tallest trees.

Rounding a bend, we stop
abruptly. Two small deer
browse in the bush,
stretching to nibble
on needles, bending to tease
grassy tufts poking through snow.
One comes nearer, and
nearer still.

See the luminous great fringed
eyes, the soft black nose
working the air, one ear cocked
at a crazy angle. Will she come closer,
does she want to?

We stand statuesque, scarcely breathing,
the moment suspended between us.
Then she turns, wanders away, and
merges with the shadowy trees.

Just for an instant, we had dared to think
we might be kin.

Grasses

Tall and supple,
their amber fronds
feather in the wind,
their lanky length
sways in the breeze,
their toes frozen
in iron ground,
packed in grubby,
week-old snow.

What do winter grasses
want? Do they seek community?
Progeny? The warmth of sun,
of shelter?

They stand and wave,
offer hope in bleak
terrain, color for the
eye, silence and
persistence.

That might be enough.

Ríme

The world is rimed today,
each twig and branch rhymes with
the other yet remains distinct
and solitary in community.
Like smoke the Swedish poplars
rise, like bones the tree behind.
A weeping birch's frosty drapes
droop and shimmer and the sun
would like to shine but hesitates
behind a pale grey cloud. To shine
would shatter all this loveliness.
It knows.

This mean and mangy sky

This mean and mangy sky
bearing down upon us
makes my stomach sour,
turns my heart into
a haunted house.

This sky squelches
passion, drains
enthusiasm, yawns
at creativity.

This sky neither rains
nor snows but hangs,
listless, a blister on
the eye, a blot on
the day.

Across the way, a bird
alights on the tip of a
sky-scrabbling spruce:
a bundle of life, a ball
of feathers, a potential of
song.

I feel a smile begin to form.

Reprieve

With just a glance
the eyes drink in
enough to slake each
thirsty sense. The sky is
painted in pastels. A few pale
brush strokes intervene.
Low sounds smudge,
insinuate instead of strident
pitches clamoring. The air feels

kind, its scent is tender.
January's hard-edged, crystal-
cornered brittleness, its icy
blocks of brilliant blue have given

way to an April softness and
our twisted limbs, our squinting
eyes release, we shed our adversarial
clothes and slip with ease into
the world's embrace.

May Snow

Snow drifts aimlessly
from a flat grey cover
of cloud.
Flakes float by my window,
are caught
in the glossy dense foliage
of freshly dressed trees,
leaves shuddering
with the cold wet weight
of their unbidden guest.

A surreal sun
sends a fiery probe,
bores a hole in the sky,
raising a light morning wind
that tumbles the trees
scattering their delicate burden.

Another sky
blue this time
nibbles at the edge
of this one.

Change is the only constant
in May.

II. Up Close
and Personal

Zander

Hair on end,
dreamy eyed,
pyjamas twisted round
his lean body,
our grandson creeps quietly
downstairs, clutching
a well-worn teddy.

"Look who's here.
Grandma and Grandpa slept over!"

Rescued from floods
the night before
we crowd our daughter's apartment.

A light dawns
in his hazel eyes.
Our grandson looks pleased
and asks if I
would like to color
with him. Of course
I would. Anything
to forget the lake
in front of our house,
the basement
filled with muck.

Out come the rainbow-colored felt pens,
paper plates to cut into masks.
Before we can even finish breakfast
we are transported
to his shiny-bright world.

My Sister, the Contemplative

She sits,
looks up,
her gaze blends
with golden mountain,
placid lake.
She sighs,
long and full.

She has no words.
She has no training,
has not read tomes
on meditation,
does not sit *zazen*,
and her limbs are not
inclined to lotus
but she sits
looks up
and sighs.

My sister,
the contemplative.

Father

You loved opera and its heroines.
The tubercular Mimi and Violetta
made tears run down your ruddy cheeks.
At least maestro Mozart's women were healthy.
How often you intoned the Contessa
forgiving her Count his peccadillos
in *Figaro's* riotous final act,
         breaking into broken song,
         emotion ravaging your voice.

You loved women.   Or hated them.
In any case they were favored with
your full attention   except the ones
who remained at home. They grew,
they blossomed, with a pat on the back
for a job well done now and then,
but never gained the stature of
a Susanna, not even a sick Violetta
         bringing tears to your eyes,
         nestled close to your heart.

Your heart, a place your daughters sought
but never seemed to attain.

Inheritance

My aunt's estate
fills a small book,
thirty-four pages
contain the tale
of what she owned,
what she gave,
and what remained
to be divided.

Named are the furnishings,
storey by storey,
in the dark house
she lived in so long.
Drapes and tapestries,
desks and tables
take their place
on a detailed list.
Even the bench
that graced the garden
does not escape
the tallying glance.

A codicil in her large clear script
names items she meant for particular people:
an old piano made by Steinway,
a coral necklace with golden clasp,
silver scissors in an ivory box.

Page after page
is covered with numbers,
calculations

before and after,
stocks and bonds and bank certificates:
so much for him
and this much for her,
and all the rest
to religious foundations.

I think of my aunt.
Vital and positive,
she was always supportive.
Behind the exterior,
buzzing with busyness,
she was perpetually seated
in full lotus pose.
Rooted, calm,
poised, compassionate,
she held those she met
in equal esteem.

The wisdom and warmth
that nurtured me,
her wide-questing spirit
that lit my way,
that is the inheritance
I received from my aunt.
She valued me as a human being.
She acknowledged my right
to a place in the world.

I close the book
on the carpets and silver,
the seals and signatures
of lawyers and notaries.

This book does not hold
my inheritance.
I *live* the legacy
my aunt left me.

Ode to My Husband

He skates, does not walk,
legs flung recklessly out,
energetic and tall
and oddly innocent
striding with confidence
through my life.

I can spot him from afar.
When he comes nearer, seeing me,
he stops and plucks a phantom guitar
and warbles a soundless serenade
that never fails to make me laugh.

I love his head, the shape of it,
so large and solid and round.
I love the hands that swallow mine,
dependable and warm.

The comfort of years together
does not stifle the delight,
the surprise at finding his love
so fresh, so constant every day
and him still hard to resist.

Sunday Morning

Sitting in your wingback chair
earphones on, you peruse
a musical score resting easily on your knees
while I muck and meddle and play
with poems I've written a while ago.
Words pass through my fingers like yarn
evoking various images
each bearing its own momentum.
Any one could take the poem
on a totally different track.

We sit enveloped by stillness
that folds around us, holds us close.
Where two or three are gathered,
we listen for music, for words,
for the weaver of our souls.

Just For a Moment

This year on
Advent Sunday
you brought the boxes
from the basement: boxes
filled with other boxes,
carefully labeled, stuffed
with tissue holding
breakable Christmas balls,
candlesticks, and angels.

We wove the garland
over the banister, wide
red ribbon anchoring it.
We hung ornaments from
the railing and as we worked
side by side I thought,
some year one of us
will do this alone.

It made me pause
and deep inside, a small
bird stopped her singing.

Then, the shortbread cookies
were done and I had to run
to the kitchen. But the
preciousness of life with you
flooded my eyes just
for a moment.

Midland Road

Midland Road is no road at all
but a meandering bit of lane
that bends among spreading granddaddy oaks
whose frayed fingers rake the sky,
hosting an unseen troupe of
lively birds on this February day.

We stop to listen to the layers of sound,
jubilant warbling broken only by
the occasional song of a robin
whose voice we know well.

While treetops hide their mysterious cache,
here below little monochrome birds
flit through a mesh of twigs as if to
divert us from their anonymous cousins.

We muse at a "House for Sale" on the other side,
imagine ourselves on a grey day,
happily ensconced within its walls,
a fire alive in the fireplace.
These trees, this birdsong would be ours.
I would write, you would study and bake bread,
and daily we would sally forth
to taste the sea air, watch the eagles
wheeling overhead...
if we lived on Midland Road.

The Kiss

Kisses were kisses
when I was young,
a custom, a habit,
even a duty.
A gathering of lips,
mouth meeting mouth
was a greeting or "thank you"
meaning little
to me.

There was a boy
in my early teens
whose kisses, like family's,
were tight and dry.
Electricity arced
from one to the other
but the kiss and the current
were unevenly matched.

Till Ralph.

When Ralph first phoned
to ask me out
a small tornado
rolled through our house.
He was a year older,
drove his dad's car
and looked like an Aztec prince
with cinnamon skin
and liquid brown eyes,

a heroic straight nose
and lovely full mouth.

He wanted to take me out!!!

I clung to the phone
breath stopped in my throat
while my parents went off
to their bedroom to talk.
I'm sure I prayed
"Please, please let me go."
When they emerged
it was "Yes," and "You may."

He appeared on the step
hair glistening with rain
in a soft grey sweater,
sleeves partly rolled up.
I remember his hand,
—my skin remembers—
his palms thickly calloused
from pumping gas
at an after-school job.
His hand rested lightly
upon my arm
awakening feelings
entirely new.

And then, his kiss.
Lips slightly parted
hovered on mine,
soft searching tongue
felt so strange, so foreign

that only his tenderness
kept me from shrinking
and shrugging away,
out of his arms.

Kisses were never the
same after that.

Neither was I.

Lunch

My friend brings lunch
but looks perturbed.
"I think I got
someone else's order," she says.

We open the bag.
Out spill individual bundles,
snug little packets,
with bagels tucked neatly
within their folds.
"Oh no," she cries, "Dijon mustard.
And where's the lettuce?
I asked for lettuce."

My friend speaks grace
over the unexpected.
We bite into fresh,
crunchy bagels, into crisp
red onions, green peppers,
cucumbers. Cream cheese
oozes out with every bite
and with it, slippery
sliced tomatoes.

Her face relaxes.
It is delicious.

What else could it be
between dear friends?

For Norma

"Mrs. Tiggywinkle"

Mrs. T
(but her name is Alice)
comes out of the shadows
to welcome us to her domain
of wondrous washers, shows us
how to load them up.
Our clothes rock merrily
back and forth as
sudsy water massages them.

Mrs. T
looks very weary.
There's no twinkle
in her eyes.
She labors days
washing for others,
then goes home to mending.

She watches me struggle
with fitted sheets,
the kind that hug
the mattress. Her sense
of neatness propels her forward.
"Let me show you how," she says.

Like a magician with his top hat
from which erupt rabbits and scarves,
Mrs. T thrusts her hand in a corner
and fits the next corner over it.
Soon her hand is gloved in layers
and with a flick of the wrist the sheet

falls into folds and she parcels it up.

A smile momentarily
lights up her eyes
as I express my delight.
The laundromat,
an adventure for me,
for her is something else.

For Alice Turlock
Mrs. Tiggywinkle is the laundress in Beatrix Potter's books

Granny Smith

Whose granny was she anyway?
Smith is such a common name.

Was she anything like
the apple? Crisp, juicy,
and mighty sour?

Where did she live
and how is it that
her name is on our
lips, we hold her in
our hands, with eager
teeth we crush her
into luscious bits
of fruity flesh?

I wonder what
she'd think of that:
  Granny Smith,
    an apple!

The Publicist and the Poet

She suggests Chapters,
or rather, that famous coffee
joint next door. I am early,
she comes late and our chit-
chat joins the generic noise.

I'm forced to read lips
though what she says is
not what I thought I was
going to hear. She bemoans
her nails, recently spoiled, when
she helped a friend to move.
In mid-sentence she tosses
her hair and complains of
its texture, the cut, and "Darn,
there's a hair in my eye!"

I try to coax her into
divulging what she, the
publicist, can do for me,
the poet, with a first book
on my hands. She whips out
photographs of her daughters.
"Lovely," I murmur, "just
like you." This piece of fatuousness,
thank God, gets lost in ideas
she has for marketing me.

In the end she rises,
taut white T-shirt
dipping dangerously, deep

tanned cleavage winks at me,
dyed blonde hair falls into place.
My last attempt to pin
her down. "I'm looking for
a game plan."

"I'll work on it this
weekend," is her confident
reply, but she is flying
to Vancouver, won't be back
till Sunday night.

Right.

Impasse

One cold November day
he stood upon our step,
a dessicated little man,
indifferent raincoat hung
upon his frame, a well-worn
satchel underneath one arm.
The plastic poppy offered some
relief, a splash of red in his
lapel and on his head, a dapper
Irish motoring cap.

He held out a tract.
I glanced upon its childish
comics, knew the text by heart:
predictions, destiny, doom, but...
in the end a few thousand saved.

We exchanged some words:
his of inquiry ("Did you
know...?"), mine of demurral
("we *can't* know") and came to
an impasse whose only solution
lay in a fond farewell.

He shuffled off,
convictions intact
and I retreated, just
the same.

I thought him kind, I thought him
dear. I would have had him in
to tea but for that well-worn satchel.

Santa Fe

No voice, no grief,
no need for ritual
that called me to
the church wall, to
the stainless steel containers
holding plastic bags of ashes
of my parents, now long gone.
Nor was I drawn
to drive once more
past the house which
had been theirs.

I did not visit,
was not tempted by
what was not there.
There was no effort,
struggle, wishful thinking,
just awareness of
sweet sunshine,
shadows cast
on adobe walls.

In this historic city my
past had turned to air and
I was free at last.

Traveler

A month of travel
and I am surprised
to find I still wear
this body whose palate
has savored several
languages and various
foods; when I've sat
baking in the sun
beneath a chestnut's leafy
fingers just above the Côte
d'Azur; I've hiked the
softly padded paths of
densely wooded Switzerland
along the Rhine, mist resting
coolly on the hills; I've plodded
through the sand dunes
on the shore of Ameland, eyes
riveted on ships and seabirds
and I've trundled onto trains
and trams with suitcases
and packs and in the muddle,
lost myself, found
myself in front of a
Van Gogh and swallowed back
my tears in the Concertgebouw's
lofty hall, Brahms' Requiem
sculpting my bones anew.

Now at last
I've come to rest
before we leave, to let

events and people
pass like film behind
my eyes, recognizing
the container that I am
is full:
fully here
and fully there
and everywhere
at home.

3:00 AM

A train is a train
is a train at
3:00 in the morning
no matter where
you are.

When sleep dangles
like stalactites from
the ceiling, never dropping
down to spread her lightly
woven web and the Goldberg

Variations spin their
gorgeous motifs over
and over in your brain,
all you want is

to escape, to catch that
fleeting train and disappear
with its horn's fast fading
sound in this early morning
no-man's land.

"*Les Rastoubles*"

Waking up midst waves of green
in many shades, my window
looking into trees whose trunks
are rooted down below where
terraces marked by walls of
undressed stone once hosted
roses, I think this house has been
ill-named. Instead of stubble,
oleanders thrive, clematis winds
its way through hedges that defy
a trimmer; olive trees and spreading
figs, thorny agave, spiky yucca
flourish in the southern sun.

The old stone house wears a coat of cream,
sheltered by a red-tiled roof and
shutters, real ones, useful in the heat
that mercilessly drills but fails to penetrate
thick walls. Walls are home to geckos,
jumping spiders, a long and slender wasp
who neatly builds a nest under the roof
with tiny beads of clay, meticulously smoothed.

At night the tree frogs
lay a carpet of sound,
antiphonal choir that starts and
stops at whim, or so it seems,
and in the chill of morning, silence
thick as mist is broken only by
the rich and various song of birds.

At the end of a narrow
winding track this house
lies well tucked away,
serene among its elderly neighbors,
inscrutable behind a wooden gate,
replete with history all its own.

"Les Rastoubles."

Les Rastoubles is a vacation home on the Riviera

Missing

The urge to travel to
exotic places, preferably
in comfort, luxury if possible
is endemic to the rich.

Weddings are no longer
ritualized in the parish of
the home-grown couple.
Everybody has to fly
to Fiji, to Jamaica,
at the very least Hawaii.

All we do is trade
one glittering resort for
another, be it here or
on the coast of Cuba.
We need never see
the local folks,
the grinding poverty
and pollution.

We have failed to love
our home. We run away
to find what's missing
in our lives and fail to see
that it is where we have been planted.
Had we loved this place
we would not now be facing
universal degradation.

Sea

Today my meditation window
reveals a slate grey sea
that has no shine,
that does not mirror or invite.
The rippled water turns away,
shunning the seeking-after-depth
that is my nature.

Today the sea does not want to be known.

I understand.
Being hidden feeds
the archives of my soul.
Knowledge builds in its busy stacks.
The library ever gathers and collects.

The sea, like me,
hides and holds
her treasure on an
overcast day.

Autumn Country

This country comes to meet me,
not shyly, not hesitantly but
with arms open wide, filled with
textured grasses, clumpy bushes, shades
of blonde and bronze and scarlet, swept

along by an icy wind off
freshly-fallen snow on Castle Mountain,
rippling, brushing, waving this brocaded
carpet, rich as any Persian rug. It comes

to meet me, all around me, flowing
through me, leaves me gasping till
the next wave, and the next. I am
drinking, eating, breathing color, gulping

air so crisp I have to chew it,
spitting rose-hips red as blood, golden
grasses liquefying in my veins and
running out my toes. This country meets
me, *is* me, in the autumn of my life.

Resolve

I'm going to celebrate
my wrinkles,
stop lamenting droops
and creases.

Let the looking glass
take note. I will not
let you stare me down
again. I'll live within
the finely folded, tender

sheath of skin that has been
mine these many years as if
it is the lovely gown created

for the ball at which the prince
met Cinderella, saw her only
with the eyes of love.

Aging

The waving water dimples
like the flesh of my belly.
My own soft aging skin
ripples, weaves and sings the same song
as the rest of creation,
puckering, gathering, creasing, folding.
Such lovely words speak of wealth
hidden
but unfurling,
spreading, flowing
over all my experience,
blessing and anointing
time passed and
the reality of now.

Ecstasy

When does ecstasy lose
its thrust, its brilliance
and become a stranger?
Oh, that sharply focused,
all inclusive one-ing, when
did it become so shy?

Like an aging mountain
ecstasy erodes, smoothes out,
its jagged peak a flowing contour.
Sitting in the third row, maybe
even further back, I watch it at
a distance, bearing in my bones
its memory.

Fall Encounter

Tawny grasses bend back and part
from our boots as strawberry runners,
rosy-leaved, spread around us like the
cracks in a broken mirror.

Further on the grove of yellow aspens
calls, a sanctuary inviting ritual.
The large old poplar that takes center stage
and blazed so brilliantly last year
is threaded throughout with dead twigs.

I rest my hand on her trunk.
We talk. I feel her voice.
She accepts life as it comes and
withered branches are but part of it.
I listen to the quiet mutter of leaves
and hear them snap as they start their descent
towards the ground.

I have but lately joined the conversation.
These trees are always chatting
from the robust rustle of summer's foliage
to the pale sparse dialogue of this late fall.
Soon they will be all but mute
except for the occasional creak and groan
of wood bending under snow.
Denied their voices they will stand
living their lives in stillness.

My eyes fill as I walk slowly away.
I've heard their goodbye in my soul.

Could this be a final parting?
Perhaps.
Like aging, it too is acceptable.
Goodbye is continually woven
into the pattern of our lives.

Liminal

The day she lay dying,
being knit into the final
stretch of her journey as
the great beyond prepared
to welcome her, snowflakes
poured from the sky, big
raggedy floppy things
weaving spring out of
winter, blooming on the
threshold in between

Spring suspended, hovering
in its tracks, thwarted by
a brittle cold despite the
swelling sun that followed

She, too, in between,
held by a thin thrall
of what-has-been and
turning slowly to
the light.

Sept. 11, 2001

This is the fall
that shattered around us
when hate
in the name of God
drilled a hole through our world
and it came shuddering,
shaking, sobbing down and
lives broke into pieces and
our masks cracked open
and we became real
and joined the mourners
because we discovered *they*
were *us*.

Universal

Tell me your story
and I will hold it
cradle it in a Papago basket
deep and light and reedy
and when it begins
to overflow I'll gather
all the bits and fragments for
you to see and say yes,
yes, that is my story.

Tell me your story
but whatever you do,
do not ask for mine.
For mine alights on every
branch, scuttles along
the desert floor, is carried
off by the least wind.
It has escaped me, is
no longer mine but that
of the universe.

Introvert

Three o'clock and I have spent
all my energy, spoken poetry
with all my heart, watched
their faces change and soften,
eyes darken with emotion,
resting in the loving cup
of words, rocking, moving,
flowing, holding.

Now the hours I did not sleep
rob me of coherence as does
all the outward flow of inter-
action. I am picking at the
last straws in the bottom of
the barrel.

Just a little longer, can you
make it, can you last
until the clock strikes four?

The Beanpot

Empty pot.
No beans.

Maybe just as well.
Had too many beans lately.

Empty pot.
No beans.

Empty me.

III. Still Breathing

breath mantra

My breath is not my breath
but Breath.

It breathes me in and
breathes me out. It passes

through this form I call
my own.

Everything is breath, is
breathed, even that which seems

without. This mountain, creamed
in snow: Big Snowy Breath,
Breath With Shoulders.

What if...

What if this one
perfect
round
breath
were all
we can know
of heaven
now?

A Swinging Door

"What we call 'I' is just a swinging door which moves
when we inhale and when we exhale."
—Shunryu Suzuki, *Zen Mind, Beginner's Mind*

I follow the swinging
door until a cosmic
wind steady and strong
holds it open and the
universe pours in and "I"
pour out and all is
stream, is wave, is
oceanic.

Why delight
in what just is and
always has been? Why
regret when swing slows
down, grinds to a halt
and "I" once more
appear?

Cosmic wind finds
ways to flow
and even "I"
am not
in the way.

Each Breath

Each breath
tall
full
blooms in the mouth,
a bowl of amber wine
from which the Holy takes
small sips.

Take one breath
mindfully.
This moment
is complete.

Beauty

I learned long ago
that beauty grasped
is beauty no longer.

To meet with beauty,
relax your grip,
bid farewell to desire,
let go of the tension

between the eyes and soften,
soften till she turns
to you.

What happens next
can only be breathed.

transience

When my breath pauses
lingers
looks around

before it rises once again
I wonder

how will it be when it pauses
lingers
looks around

and fails to rise again?

Faithful effort will subside
into universal breath.

Not with lungs
will I be breathed.

Prayer

Oh Lord, sweeten
my mouth, soften
my eyes, strengthen
my heart, that I not
succumb to the world's
woes, my own weakness,
and the apparent hopelessness
of things.

Longing

O Beloved
there is such an
unsightly lump of
longing in me. What
am I to do?

"My longing is
your longing. Take
and eat and be
at home."

Together then, we sit,
well fed.

Something Else?

May I crawl inside
now, touch upon

that tremulous membrane,
fine fiber covering of

spirit, lift its weave
and find you there?

In the dark wine of
your presence, may I

flow, may I sip,
shudder, breathe, melt?

Or is there something else
you would have me do?

Lord

Lord
I want to be
so empty of self
and even of this
want, that only your
voice will be heard
within me.

Time

Twenty minutes for meditation.
So I think.
Time has other ideas,
spreads her wings,
flies silently away,
leaves me sitting
in a field that knows nothing
of time, has never been touched
by it.

Gone is my secure companion,
one I rail against but one
who often rescues me,
for who can question
Time's authority?

Later, when I rise from prayer
all I taste is timelessness.

Lectio with Leaves

Take this patch
of tawny grasses,
strawberry leaves threading
throughout, leaves as red
as their fruit in another
season; many-petaled sage-grey
lichen, smaller than the tip of your
finger; miniature ferns, green
and sturdy, and bleached-blond horsetail
with stems like bamboo; stone flaked off
a nearby mountain millions of years ago.

Take this sacred bit of ground
and read it, inwardly digest it,
contemplate the exquisite detail,
multiply by infinity and you will have
the sum of this precious earth.

Make space in your heart for her.
Vow to live accordingly.

Lectio divina is prayerful reading of scripture

Lectio with Mountain Peak

Every moment
earth and sky conspire
to create a different view
though this mountain never moves.

Last night's snow
has pulled in clouds
and wispy mist that flow,
though slowly, over her
concealing now her crags and canyons,
now her sharp-etched silhouette.

When sun breaks through
her lower slopes assume
a glow of amber aspens
as her summits blaze
intensely white.

I could sit, day in, day
out, through every season
of the year and never would
this prayer grow tired
or its richness dull.

The Witness

When I witness transformation,
huge change in a moment of time,...

    a body riddled
    with angles and corners
    and edges so sharp
    they would surely cut;
    a throat so blocked,
    a voice pulled tight
    and full of gravel,
    (she sits as if
    the chair won't hold her,
    hovers just above the seat)

Then

    a story told,
    a wound revealed,
    a breath of air
    (the Spirit passing)
    and eyes darken,
    the body sinks
    into the chair,
    edges soften,
    the voice clears,
    all the angles melt into curves

...and I myself am changed.

Another Story

Her story, says the wind
in passing, is not yours
to tell, much less to hold.
Let it go into my keeping,
I will be its treasurer.

Take mine too then, I'll not
need it, is my message
to the wind. For some time now
details of that heavy
tome have lost their luster.
Every body has a story.
I am growing lighter
till at last the wind will
clothe me with herself and
hers will be the only
story.

Listen

If you give me
the post of listener
I will listen to
the river careen
over rocks, down cliffs,
and as it pools beneath
old trees.

I will listen to
the woodpecker's mantra,
to the red-breasted nuthatch's
squeezed *quack-quack*,
to the song sparrow's long
and lyrical line.

I will listen to
the breeze as it rumples the
leaves, to the storm wind's
menacing roar.

If you call me your
listener I promise to listen
deeply and well until
the end.

Do You Think?

Do you think when
you come before God
armored with books
fortressed with intellect
you will want to parse
Saint Paul, consult the
Hebrew texts, maybe even
the Greek?

Perhaps you would.

Face down on the ground
I will lie forever, no
thing to commend me unless
the Holy desires to see
my face, lift me out of
the dust to his arms,
his lips, his heart.

Don't

Why not write about prayer?
the author asks.

Why not *not*? Why not
just enter our lives fully?

That will be enough.
Let's be planted wholly

in the depths, the heights,
the breadth of our lives,

the life of the world,
each agonizing moment.

Let's, for God's sake, not
write about it.

Lent

Each year when
winter drags her mangy
tail, Lent breaks in.

With her comes
anticipation. The heart
stirs, the spirit spreads
her wings. I hear
the call that echoes down
the ages from the church.

   Come.

How can I come?
Your bricks, your rafters,
every part of you is torn
by violence and dissension.
At the heart of every
battle your self-righteousness
holds court.

   Come.

I would love to
come, to sit in holy
silence, hold the cup in
reverent hands. Each year

I am torn. Then I hear
the geese arrive, watch

the spring snow drive
across the lake.

The only ritual that
can claim me is the
world's wild gift of
life, ever-changing,
not-excusing, holding
out her ample arms.

Then I sit
in holy silence,
hold the cup
in reverent hands.

good friday

What does the spine know?

lashes, beatings,
unbearable weight
pulling apart

A river of life
a flow of bone
a coursing of blood
the pulse
that keeps upright
the stretch
that makes tall

bent, bowed
crunched, broken
crumbled staff
shattered rock
splintered wood

flecks of light
shredded breath
hooded dark

The spine surrenders
knows no more.

Luke thirteen: eleven

Women of the world,
    burdened and blessed
    and bent over,
    carrying their babes on their backs,
    bearing the fire,
        lighting the fire,
            sustaining the fire,
             being on fire
               in
               pain
               passion
               misery
               joy

I am woman.
        I know the journey
        through the heart
        through the womb
        into the universe
        weaving the web
        night and day
        awake and asleep

One day we give to God
        this fabulous fabric
        of many threads,
        strong as silk,
          saying,
        "It is finished..."

,

And God says,
    is always saying
        "It is good.
        It is good.
        It
        is
        very
        good."

The Path

When you have followed the map
which is not a map

and created the path with every
step

you will traverse the in-ferno,
meet the dragons and find them
tame.

You will bathe in
the pool of the past and empty it.

You will cross the desert and
fall in love with life teeming there

and you will emerge where
the luminous world swoons at your
feet, seeking what only you
can give.

and then...

And then... then I walk away
from ten- thousand thousand
words, images, interpretations
and walk into
a limitless field where I
appear, a tiny, ground-hugging
flower...or maybe not, and
You the indigo cover of
cloud, a vast intimate
silence....

Who Is God Now?

Rain.
  The drops, the spaces between,
  the times when it does not
rain.

Wind.
  When it blows, storms, rages,
  when it lies down in quiet pools.
Wind.

Body.
  When it rises strong and free, entwines with another,
  when it loses its luster and begins the long descent.
Body.

Love.
  In all its facets, birthing, growing, yearning,
  breaking, losing.
Love.

Who is God now?

Far and near.
Here, not here.

Always, all ways.
God.

IV. The Poem That Awaits

Open

In the midst of dusting, dishes,
laundry, poetry beckons and I
read and sink and notice that
small hidden door within spring

open, pushing aside tangled vine
and prickly brush that cling, that
obfuscate, and sink ever deeper

into soul, into the stillest
landscape that appears between
the outbreath and the pursuant

inhalation. This is where the
moment opens, slowly loosing and
releasing petals till the radiant

flower's heart emerges, graced
and gracious and as all-embracing
as the universe.

Instruments

"Be emptier and cry like reed instruments cry.
Emptier, write secrets with the reed pen."*

Reed instruments only cry
when breathed:
emptiness full of air.

If I could write with a reed pen
I would write only air. I
would write only breath.

Jesus breathed upon his friends,
made them instruments of his cry.

Let my pen be the empty reed,
emptier still but for that cry.

*Rumi, from "Fasting"
The Essential Rumi, p. 69
C. Barks with J. Moyne

Waiting: Holy Saturday

I have not yet written
the poem that awaits me:
    the one that will be
    so alive it bursts out
    from the pages, scattering
    shreds of paper everywhere.

    The one that curls the
    paper's edges, singeing them
    with fire, the one that
    cannot be contained and
    just like Jesus, breaks
    its bonds to stride out
    in the new spring of the world.

I may never write it.

But I shall wait with
longing and with dread
anticipation for that poem
to emerge.

Sentence

I live between
the bookends of
a lyrical phrase.

In the vastness
between the first word
and the far-in-the-distance
punctuation, I work, I dance,
I play, I love.

One ought to be able
to express
a life well lived
in a simple phrase.
Like a Zen *koan*,
each word uncovers
another layer.

Ever dropping deeper,
one would never
have to come
to the period
at the end.

Gap

I look
I listen as
poetry forms—
an unspoken place
between two breaths.

No Poem

Forget I wrote this.
I did not.
All I did was
sit with fingers loosely
wrapped around a
thick ceramic mug whose
contents warm more than
my hands; whose weight
drops wordlessly into
my body, every part;
whose rich dark brew
speaks nothing, merely
sits within the cup as
surely as a dark
sweet nectar stirs within
my soul.

Too Much

One can read
too much poetry—
stuffed to the gills
with war and sorrow
or with evening's golden light
floating on a silent lake.

Poems need
to be absorbed,
sifted,
  chewed
and swallowed, slowly,
while attending
their descent
to the body's
nether regions
where they may
take root.

Poetry Hangover

I awoke this morning
(or had I even slept?)
with a head as heavy
as the Oxford Annotated
Bible and with just as
many words and phrases
leaping around my brain.

It's the morning after
with a mouthful of
wool where last night poetry
swelled and spoke in
elegant cadences, lyrical tones.
It is as if

the whole night long
those poems kept "begatting"
as in those biblical genealogies
and now my head is splitting
with descendants, a multitude
of poetic offspring.

My poems

are not yours and sometimes
when I have fed richly
on the poetry of others I
return to my own like
a nursemaid to her foundlings.

I am not devoid of language.
I can roll out long descriptive
phrases, fat and luscious words
but then I pare them down
and excise many, left with only
a few in the end.

I am attracted to the spare
like to a tree in winter. A
winter tree dances naked,
leafless branches cradle sky.
My poems are the branches,
not important in themselves
unless they cause you to surrender
to the grand embrace of sky.

Mary O.

She witnesses but
more than that
she reaches out to
touch, and fearlessly. Then her
body, all alive and shimmering
mingles with the other/Other and
the ecstatic poet is born again and
again. Her words, though sober,
ordinary words have captured nothing
but set free the glistening, rushing wind,
the wind that slips between and through the
narrowest crack, the tightest lintel, and the dried
and withered soul breathes and blossoms once again.

On reading
"The Poet Goes to Indiana"
Mary Oliver

Pulse

Her poem is
a pulse of rain,
perfect in its
wet container.

When it meets
the waiting earth
it is enough
to water the least
alpine violet,
the most voluptuous
woodland iris.

Rainer Maria Rilke

Some mornings the world is all a-flap,
ragged and unraveling. The night
was restless, yesterday's tangles
still brood darkly in the light.

Yet weariness from lack of sleep
and the taste of that obscure fruit
that is Rilke's poetry create a point
of silence deep within.

If we ask "Why?"
it is a short path to despair

but if we stay in stillness
leaving thought and word behind,
we may be found by the eternal.

For T. M.

Thomas Merton, you're a fool, a
flamboyant fool. With flags flying
and wimples waving you
turned yourself inside out
and wrote with crayons across the sky
in letters big as life everything
that ever crossed your mind
or peopled your heart
or terrorized your sleep.

With a window on the world,
and a wary, weary, tear-stained soul
you preached and taught and soothed
and shouted, lullabied and loved
your way into our hearts.

What a fool, Thomas Merton,
such a fool for the God you loved.

Thanks for being who you were.
It makes it easier to be me.

Dylan Thomas

Shawling out of the fertile
ground of Dylan's creativity,
out of a life spent with an ear
bent close to earth's pulse,
sea and sky, making love to
love, his creamy muscular
language pours. Cradling
words and bringing them to his
lips he kissed them into the
world and watched them all
slip away, drowned in the suds
of endless celebration. Or was it
sorrow? Then the lights went out.

In the darkest time of year
I read *A Child's Christmas in Wales*.
I bite into its buttery crust, taste and
see the night sky light up, bursting into
flame as Dylan rides in triumph by.

Wild Ones

Every poet must unbind
his hair, her hair, like Rapunzel,
swing it east, swing
it west, mingle it with
the mops of other poets,
Dylan's red, Rilke's auburn,
till its great unruly mass
rises like smoke towards the sun
and burns, incandescent, sending showers
of ashes, sparks of poems dropping back
to earth.

V. Birds I Have Known

Back Again

From winter's silent,
empty skies they fly,
streaking powerfully
across the lake to land
upon the opposite shore,
surveying their domain.

The geese are back.
As are the gulls and crows.

The air's alive with
sound, with song, with
eager calls and we, who
had forgotten that it could
be so, stretch and shake our
stiff and wintry wings and find
ourselves with softer, more melodious
voices, visited by grace.

Cormorant

Out of the corner
of my eyes, I see
a glossy black wing in flight.
The cormorant,
the cormorant is back.
From room to room
I pursue him, window
to window, as he lands
in flappy water,
rises, circles,
circles the lake
twice and in a straight
unmistakable trajectory
flies away to my cries:
don't *go,* don't *go*!

Pelican

Paddling in, a tall ship,
sails unfurled and startling
white, a pelican comes around

the bend of our small lake,
a throwback, surely, to
an age when great wings darkened

the terrain where huge
beasts roamed. The family
of geese pull back to higher

ground while baby golden-
eyes pop up and under water
unaffected by the stranger

that has splashed down in
their midst. Perhaps he took
a wrong turn, blown off course.

In any case, his stay is
short. We see him, flash
of white, alight on giant

wings, take off and not
come back as we turn to one
another, eyes impassioned,

saying, "Did you see?
Have you ever...? Did
you feel...?"

Yes.

Priest

A great high priest
is the great blue heron
though not of the order
of Melchizedek.

He presides over
a water-borne parish
and should a fish pop up to
the surface, the prayer-like stance
of the heron erupts. A
ferocious bow and a snap
of his bill and this silver-scaled
Jonah descends in the dark.

One likes to think
when he resumes
his priestly pose
the great blue heron
offers thanks.

Question For the World

A polka-dotted lake.
Bleached gulls scattered
on its surface
like bones
in Ezekiel's field.

Will they come together
or persist in their
quarrelsome ways?

Mallard

Hunkered low in
the water, looking oh
so sinister, the mallard
shoots forward on
the heels of another
till both take flight,
spin into the air like
just-released tops.

And don't even *think*
of coming back! He
chases the duck to
the far end of sky,
protecting his brown,
home-spun lady, the
mother of his progeny.

Ruddy Duck

In mid June
he appeared, a

short squat tugboat,
baby's bath toy, with

the blue sky caught
in his broad bill and

a body the color of
a blood orange with

a fan of black tail
feathers, stiff and straight.

So compact and dapper
he looked but it was

his stunning blue bill
so generously scooped into

the Buddha's smile
that caused bubbles of

joy to surface, shivers
of sheer delight that

here on our lake, and
I happened to see it,

the ruddy duck had appeared.

Loon

loon
low in the water
back like a bridal
veil dotted with
pearls, shimmering

loon
elegant diver
Water parts without
ruffle or splash

loon
sleek like a fish
and just as agile
swims under water,
his shadow following
like a twin

loon
under water
gone!
Where to?

Maybe China

Exceptions

The giraffe of birds is
the great blue heron:
gawky, angular, awkward.

Except
when standing in quiet
waters, peering intently,
listening.

Except
in flight when great wings
pour from powerful shoulders,
slowly, rhythmically through
bright air.

Awkward, angular,
elegant.

Visitors

Thirty-one cormorants land
in a wedge, slice
through water, come up with
their heads held high,
black mantles spread.

Thirty-one cormorants scout
and scour one end of the lake
to the other and finding it less
than adequate, abort their tour
in quick succession, leaving the
lone loon unperturbed,
red eye unblinking,
still enthroned.

Changeling

Great blue heron
stands illumined by
a setting sun

curtsies slowly, grace-
fully, but not to us.
Eyes never lifting,
neck collapses into

shoulders, changing
him into a squat and
dowdy any-kind-of-bird.

No fish surfaces.

Long lithe neck unfolds
and rises and before us stands
a dancer, tall and slender,
in a tutu trailing feathers.

One never knows
when one may meet
at twilight's edge
another Nureyev.

Rudolph Nureyev, the famous Russian ballet dancer

Too Many Herons

Too many herons,
  says the poet
gathering poems
for a book. But
do you suppose
they'd cooperate?
Each one thrusts
a skinny leg forward,
prances about, showing
off, they crowd around
like eager kids: *choose
me, choose me!*
I have to call them
to order, sternly. Obediently,
  they fall into line,
leaving slimy, spidery tracks
all over my pristine pages,
every one to be included.

Unexpected

We perch among
the treetops on
the fifth floor where

our nearest neighbor
is a giant nest,
deserted now.

Clouds shift and curl,
producing rain, then
hail, and in between

a momentary hummingbird.
Red epaulettes explode from
his black wings and we

we, wishing to be
hibiscus blooms, at
the very least, a trumpet vine.

Waxwing

A solitary waxwing
clings tenaciously
to a birch branch,
thrown to and fro
by each gust of wind.
Spherical, feather-plumped,
she prevails against
the bouncing, icy air.

Standing straight out
from her soft grey body,
an oar, a flag
of orange, ochre, and
white keeps her upright
on windy waves.

Why do you stay,
hang on so doggedly?
What is it you see
from your precarious perch?
What wisdom (or foolishness)
makes you persist all alone,
you light and lively creature?

King

The granddaddy of all ravens
with a beak like midnight
and the eye of a lighthouse
struts back and forth
as if he were king,
king of this peeling picnic table,
sovereign of leftovers,
garbage and carrion.

And none would question
his royalty when he takes
to the sky on polished black wings
making lazy circles
over mountain summits
and broad-backed valleys
leaving us earthbound creatures, so
heavily shod, to imagine what
that could be like.

Magpies

They pour out of the south
into the dawn which wraps herself
in low-slung shawls, luminous,
warm, inviting.

They swarm like giant butterflies,
steered by ruffled rudders,
buoyed by winter air. Theirs is

the only movement on this first day
of the year, on a frozen landscape tucked
in last night's slumber, snuggled up to
last year's dreams.

Merlin

He sat unflinching
in the tree, indifferent
to its brilliant leaves
and small red apples.
All the afternoon he sat.

I thought to wave him
off. A threat to song birds,
I wanted him gone. I
stepped outside, he
fixed me with his
amber gaze. Nailed
to the step, I came all apart

in the net of his unrelenting
stare. In the end it was *I*
who fled, was forced to endure
his presence till at last he
spread his wings with ease and
flew away.

Ten years later
I still see
those eyes.

Woodpeckers

An unholy trinity,
three gorgeously ugly
woodpeckers fly
over our heads,
keen sense of direction, aiming for
the crippled remains of
a once-glorious birch.

Three feathered clowns
clamped to the trunk
peer about with cocky
eyes, craning their skinny necks.
Now the ritual drums begin,
strong beaks hammering, cherry-red
crests catching the sun.

Think I would ever change
places with even one?

Just try me!

Raven

If I were to be
other than I am
I would like to be
a raven, big,
dark and strong, like
the one whose deep voice
calls across the valley, whose
loose and loping flight is
matched by none, whose
great wings part the air
whap-whack
who rises high above the forest,
lands on sun-drenched rocks
surveying all
the earth. If I were
to be
other than I am
I would be
a raven.

Epilogue

Eternal

If this is all there is,
you know, when this
magical body folds and
its shine slowly creeps
away, if this is all
there is, it may very well
be fine.

Who knows what eternity is?

Something of me is indelibly marked
on the wind and the soil, in the
song of a robin and the curve
of a petal, in the word that goes forth.

If that is all there is
it may well be
truly fine.

LaVergne, TN USA
26 March 2010
177323LV00001B/9/P